Portable File-Folder Word Walls

20 Reproducible Patterns for Thematic Word Walls
to Help Children Become Better Readers, Writers & Spellers

by Mary Beth Spann

New York ☀ Toronto ☀ London ☀ Auckland ☀ Sydney

Mexico ☀ New Delhi ☀ Hong Kong

Dedication

With love and admiration to Betty Moskowitz—an inspiring teacher
and mentor who touches children and adults alike with her warmth,
sensitivity and intelligence. You are so brilliant, Betty,
you make the near-impossible look easy. — MBS

Acknowledgments

Many thanks to talented illustrator, Rusty Fletcher, and to my
ingenious editor, Liza Charlesworth, who thought up the idea of
file-folder word walls in the first place. — MBS

Cover design by Jaime Lucero
Interior design by Grafica, Inc.
Cover and Interior Illustrations by Rusty Fletcher
ISBN: 0-439-05181-9

Printed in the U.S.A.

Contents

Introduction

Welcome to the wonderful world of *Portable File-Folder Word Walls*! This book contains patterns for creating 20 easy-to-make file-folder word walls, which when assembled, will stand up on their own like greeting cards. The shapes are perfect for collecting and displaying thematic-inspired vocabulary words. All you need do is duplicate the shape on a copying machine, mount on the front of a file-folder, then trim along the dash lines. The inside of the file-folder is then ready for you to record a word bank of theme-based vocabulary words, while the back cover can feature story starter suggestions.

The beauty of these word walls is that they are portable—they can be displayed on tabletops, transported to and from desks and learning centers, or popped into a self-sealing bag for take-home writing projects. With consistent usage, you'll discover your file-folder word walls help improve students' spelling skills and vocabulary development, while adding intrigue and interest to the writing process. They're easy to make and fun to use, so begin making your collection of stand-up word walls today!

Super-Easy Word Wall How-To's

1. Duplicate the desired shape on a copying machine. For an attractive, sturdy cover consider copying the shape onto colored construction paper that best matches the theme and design of the word wall (e.g., orange for the Perky Pumpkin, pink for Pink Piggy Bank, etc.).

2. Use craft glue or rubber cement to mount the shape onto the front of a file-folder, being careful to align edges labeled "fold edge" and "folder opens here" with corresponding folder edges. Trim top of shape along dash lines.

3. Color and decorate the cover and label. (Look for specific Quickie Decorating Tips offered with each word wall model.)

4. Open the folder and use this space to copy the word wall title and then record vocabulary words related to the theme. For example, you might write the words *snowman*, *icicle*, *mittens*, etc. beneath the title "Our Winter Words."

5. If you wish to offer students story starter suggestions, close the folder and glue the label reading "Our _____ Story Starters" to the top of the back cover. Use remaining space on this back cover to record more story starters suggested by you or your students.

Quickie Decorating Tips

Look to these tips for instant ideas to add sparkle to your designs! Short on time? Parents unable to volunteer in the classroom may be eager to construct word walls with special decorative touches.

Introducing File-Folder Word Walls

1. Prepare one or more of the portable word walls. Share these with your class. Point out how these word walls are portable mini-versions of the full-size word walls you may be displaying on the walls in your classroom. Show how each shape suggests target words you will be recording inside. Note the title and cover details together. Talk with the class about the importance of handling the word walls with care.

2. Open the word wall to show how the title appears again inside.

3. Have children brainstorm words related to the topic.

4. Record children's suggestions on a large piece of chart pad paper. Then, as the class looks on, transfer these to the inside of the word wall. Decide together which words can be illustrated, and then invite volunteers to insert small drawings next to these words.

5. Using a clean piece of chart pad paper, model how to write a story using some of the words recorded in the file-folder word bank. During this process, invite student input. "Think out loud" as you formulate what you are going to write. In this way, children can observe how you refer to the word lists both for inspiration and accurate spelling.

Putting File-Folder Word Walls to Work in Your Classroom

1. Walk children through any procedures you decide upon, such as how to access, handle, and store your file-folder word walls.

2. Develop and display a collection of your file-folder word walls.

3. Demonstrate how children may enrich writing attempts by using word walls in conjunction with other related materials such as thematic literature, bulletin boards, games, manipulatives, take-home backpacks, etc.

4. Store word walls in a box located at your writing center. Students may then borrow word walls from the center and use them at their desks. Word walls may also be tacked to a bulletin board, displayed on a learning center table top, or clipped to a clothesline strung across the room. (**Tip:** Try making multiple copies of each file-folder word wall so more than one child at a time can work with the same collection of words.)

5. Build in ways for children to share their word wall-inspired writings. You may, for example, ask children to read writings aloud, provide a bulletin board for children to post writings on, or publish pieces in a class journal.

6. Encourage children with particular interest to create, design, and decorate original file-folder word walls complete with words and story starters for classmates to use.

Pairing Story Starters With File-Folder Word Walls

Use your portable word walls to record theme-related story starters. Simply copy and cut out the story starter label provided with each shape and glue this to the top of the back outside cover of the word wall. In the remaining space, add your own original story starters to inspire your young writers.

Back-to-School Bus

BEEP—BEEP! Time to take a trip on this friendly bus and generate some school-inspired vocabulary along the way!

Suggested Word List

- bus
- bus driver
- school
- teacher
- backpack
- learn
- pencil
- crayons
- paper
- work
- principal
- reading
- writing
- math
- science
- social studies
- gym
- play
- circle time
- lunch box
- friends
- books

Cover Decorating Tip

▶ Cut two circles the same size as the bus wheels from file-folder scraps. Use brass fasteners to attach these "turnable tires" to the bus shape.

Story Starters

▶ Cut and paste your story starters onto the back of your word wall folder for instant writing ideas.

Our Back-to-School Bus Story Starters

☼ Describe your school day.

Tell which school activities you like best and why.

☼ If you were in charge of the school, what would you change? Why?

Our School Words

folder opens here

Back-to-School Bus
COVER
TEMPLATE

Happy Apple Tree

Suggested Word List

- apple
- apples
- tree
- branch
- basket
- pick
- seeds
- core
- skin
- pie
- stem
- sweet
- crunchy
- red
- green
- golden
- harvest
- ripe
- crisp
- peel
- cider
- yummy

This sweet-as-apple-pie tree will help children "pick" all the right words they need to write about apples, harvest, and much more!

Cover Decorating Tip

▶ Use red, green, and brown puff-paints to "emboss" apples, leaves, and bark details on the tree.

Story Starter

▶ Cut and paste your story starter onto the back of your word wall folder for an instant writing idea.

Our Apple Story Starter

Tell about an apple memory. Have you ever picked apples, or baked a special apple recipe? To make your writing come alive for your readers, think about what you saw, heard, tasted, touched, and felt.

10

Our Apple Words

folder opens here

Weather Window

Our Weather Words

G lance out your window, then brainstorm a flurry of weather words together!

Suggested Word List

sun

sunny

clouds

cloudy

wind

windy

rain

rainy

snow

snowy

fog

foggy

humid

thermometer

temperature

meteorologist

hot

cold

cool

warm

umbrella

puddle

Cover Decorating Tip

▶ Invite kids to draw a different weather scene in each of the four window panes. For window curtains, pleat and staple fabric scraps along the top edges of the window. Tiny pieces of ribbon or yarn can serve as curtain tie-backs.

Story Starters

▶ Cut and paste your story starters onto the back of your word wall folder for instant writing ideas.

Our Weather Story Starters

☺ Tell about favorite things you do in different types of weather.

☺ Tell about a time you were not ready for a change in the weather.

folder opens here

Our Weather Words

Home Sweet Home

Our Family Words

T his word wall conjures up warm and cozy images of family. . . and family tales to tell!

Suggested Word List

- family
- home
- house
- mother
- father
- sister
- brother
- son
- daughter
- grandmother
- grandfather
- aunt
- uncle
- cousin
- relatives
- older
- younger
- child
- grown-up
- pet
- care
- love

Cover Decorating Tip

▶ Cut house pieces (windows, door, roof, etc.) from colorful craft foam. Glue pieces in place. Use waterproof fineline markers to draw on details.

Story Starter

▶ Cut and paste your story starter onto the back of your word wall folder for an instant writing idea.

Our Family Story Starter

Describe the people in your family. Tell what each person does best. Or, write about a special day you spent with one or all of your family members.

Our Family Words

folder opens here

Perky Pumpkin

Our Halloween Words

Suggested Word List

- pumpkin
- Jack-o-lantern
- orange
- patch
- bat
- spider
- witch
- ghost
- ghoul
- goblin
- monster
- skeleton
- frighten
- scare
- costume
- mask
- trick or treat
- bag
- candy
- sweet
- apple
- parade

This favorite seasonal shape helps turn pumpkin words into story seeds!

Cover Decorating Tip

▶ Use green and gold puff-paints to outline pumpkin and vine details.

Story Starter

▶ Cut and paste your story starter onto the back of your word wall folder for an instant writing idea.

Our Halloween Story Starter

Write out step-by-step directions for carving a pumpkin into a Jack-O-Lantern. Tell about any special touches you like to add to your Jack-O-Lantern. How do you make your Jack-O-Lantern light up?

Our Halloween Words

folder opens here

Merry Mayflower

This ship-shape word wall helps students set sail on a voyage toward Thanksgiving tales old and new!

Suggested Word List

- **Pilgrims**
- **Native Americans**
- **Mayflower**
- **ship**
- **voyage**
- **Plymouth Rock**
- **New World**
- **settle**
- **Columbus**
- **harvest**
- **turkey**
- **feast**
- **cranberry sauce**
- **gravy**
- **potatoes**
- **stuffing**
- **pumpkin pie**
- **corn**
- **bread**
- **celebrate**
- **thanks**
- **love**

Cover Decorating Tip

▶ Cut details (sails, ship, etc.) from colorful craft foam. Glue pieces in place. Use a black fineline marker to print lettering on foam.

Story Starters

▶ Cut and paste your story starters onto the back of your word wall folder for instant writing ideas.

Our Thanksgiving Story Starters

☼ Tell some special ways you and your family celebrate Thanksgiving.

☼ Tell what you are most thankful for this year and why.

Our Thanksgiving Words

folder opens here

Jolly Snowman

Our Winter Words

Let our jolly snowman help students pile up lots of wintry words!

Cover Decorating Tip

▶ Use a waterproof fineline marker to outline cover lettering. Brush entire snowman with a wash of watered-down white glue. While still wet, sprinkle with translucent glitter. Cut snowman details (hat, mittens, scarf, nose, eyes, mouth, etc.) from colorful fun foam or felt. Glue in place.

Story Starter

▶ Cut and paste your story starter onto the back of your word wall folder for an instant writing idea.

Suggested Word List

- snowman
- snow
- snowy
- snowing
- snowball
- ice
- icy
- icicle
- cold
- freeze
- freezing
- white
- build
- carrot
- coal
- sticks
- buttons
- scarf
- mittens
- hat
- thaw
- melt

Our Snow Story Starter

What would you do if a snowman (or snow woman) you built came to life? What would you play together? What would happen if you invited your frosty friend inside to meet your family?

Our Winter Words

Happy Heart

Our Valentine's Words

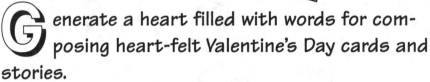enerate a heart filled with words for composing heart-felt Valentine's Day cards and stories.

Cover Decorating Tip

▶ Cut heart from red or pink craft foam. Use a black pen to print lettering on foam. Use a hot glue gun to add an edging of lace around heart.

Story Starters

▶ Cut and paste your story starters onto the back of your word wall folder for instant writing ideas.

Suggested Word List

heart
red
pink
Valentine
card
envelope
greeting
message
friend
friendship
write
poem
candy
flowers
chocolate
like
love
sweet
arrow
Cupid
secret
surprise

Our Valentine's Story Starters

☼ Tell about a special Valentine surprise you received.

☼ What special surprise would you like to prepare for someone else? In what other ways do you show love to the people you care about?

Happy Heart
COVER
TEMPLATE

folder opens here

Our Valentine's Words

Radiant Rainbow

Our Color Words

Suggested Word List

- rainbow
- red
- orange
- yellow
- green
- blue
- purple
- white
- black
- brown
- tan
- gold
- silver
- turquoise
- paint
- crayons
- color
- draw
- beautiful
- lovely
- bright
- spectrum

This word wall invites students to enliven their writing with color-full language!

Cover Decorating Tip

Use tempera paints to color the rainbow. Use a waterproof fineline marker to reprint cover lettering. Brush entire rainbow with a wash of watered-down white glue. While still wet, sprinkle with translucent glitter. (When recording the color words *inside* the word wall, record each color using the corresponding colored pencil or marker.)

Story Starters

Cut and paste your story starters onto the back of your word wall folder for instant writing ideas.

Our Color Story Starters

☼ What is your favorite color of all?

Tell why.

☼ Tell a colorful, pretend tale about discovering the treasure at the end of the rainbow.

Radiant Rainbow
COVER
TEMPLATE

Our Color Words

folder opens here

Rainy Day Umbrella

A shower of wet weather words turns a rainy day into a writer's workshop!

Suggested Word List

- rain
- rain coat
- rain hat
- hood
- boots
- umbrella
- drip
- drizzle
- sprinkle
- shower
- pour
- puddle
- splish
- splash
- damp
- wet
- drench
- thunder
- lightning
- storm
- window
- play

Cover Decorating Tip

▷ Use puff-paints to outline the umbrella's ribs and handle.

Story Starter

▷ Cut and paste your story starter onto the back of your word wall folder for an instant writing idea.

Our Rainy Day Story Starter

Tell about how you make the best of a rainy day. Where do you go? How do you dress to go out in the rain? Do you like to spend rainy days with others or alone? Why?

Our Rainy Day Words

folder opens here

Giant Dinosaur

Empower young writers by generating a long list of larger-than-life dinosaur words!

Cover Decorating Tip

▶ Add googlie eyes and purple puff-paint details.

Story Starter

▶ Cut and paste your story starter onto the back of your word wall folder for an instant writing idea.

Suggested Word List

dinosaur
big
huge
stomp
egg
hatch
extinct
scales
spikes
claws
crest
tail
teeth
Tyrannosaurus
Stegosaurus
Brachiosaurus
museum
bones
fossils
skeleton
paleontologist
dig

Our Dinosaur Story Starter

Tell what you think happened to make the dinosaurs extinct. What should we do to make sure today's endangered animals do not become extinct?

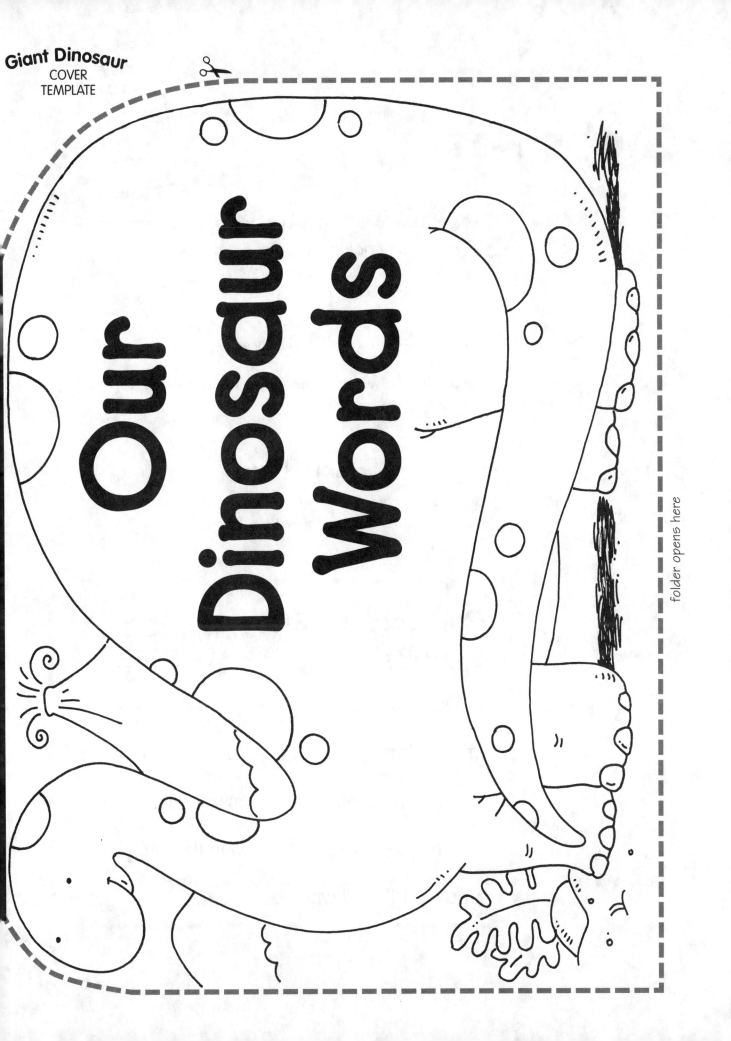

Our Dinosaur Words

folder opens here

Our Cooking Words

Chef's Hat

Suggested Word List

cook
bake
stove
oven
microwave
refrigerator
bowl
stir
boil
heat
spoon
pot
pan
spatula
whip
blender
chop
cut
chef
recipe
delicious
eat

Grab this chef's hat and whip up a delicious menu of cooking-inspired words!

Cover Decorating Tip

▶ Use black or silver puff-paint to outline hat details.

Story Starters

▶ Cut and paste your story starters onto the back of your word wall folder for instant writing ideas.

Our Cooking Story Starters

☀ Describe how to make a favorite family recipe. Tell how it looks, tastes, smells and sounds as you cook.

☀ What's your favorite food in the whole wide world? Tell why you love it.

Our Cooking Words

Spiffy Spider

Our Creepy Crawly Words

Suggested Word List

- spider
- web
- caterpillar
- butterfly
- cocoon
- ladybug
- ant
- bee
- grasshopper
- fly
- fire fly
- mosquito
- cricket
- bite
- land
- sting
- bite
- crawl
- plants
- leaves
- eggs
- wings
- flutter

Use this spider word wall to help weave a web of creepy crawly words.

Cover Decorating Tip

▶ Use black puff-paint to draw on spider details. Glue on googlie eyes.

Story Starters

▶ Cut and paste your story starters onto the back of your word wall folder for instant writing ideas.

Our Creepy Crawly Story Starters

☼ Describe your favorite insect. Tell why this insect would or would not make a good pet.

☼ Tell why you do or don't like spiders.

Our Creepy Crawly Words

folder opens here

Dapper Dog

Our Pet Words

Suggested Word List

dog
puppy
bark
cat
kitten
meow
bird
fish
hamster
gerbil
rabbit
snake
aquarium
cage
pet shop
food
dish
brush
toys
veterinarian
care
love

This playful pup will help generate pet words children can use when creating real and imagined animal tales!

Cover Decorating Tip

▷ Use bits of felt to add spots to dog. Also, glue on googlie eyes.

Story Starter

▷ Cut and paste your story starter onto the back of your word wall folder for an instant writing idea.

Our Pet Story Starter

Tell a true or fictitious story

about how a real or pretend pet came to live

with you. Include lots of details about how

you care for the pet.

folder opens here

Our Pet Words

Friendly Fish

Our Ocean Words

(G)LUB—GLUB! Our Friendly Fish invites children to dive into a sea of underwater words.

Suggested Word List

fish
octopus
whale
shark
dolphin
jellyfish
starfish
water
seaweed
waves
coral
beach
sand
shells
tides
boat
ship
dive
diver
float
swim
swimmer

Cover Decorating Tip

▷ Glue on a googlie eyes. Dress up the fish by adding color felt to its fins and stripes.

Story Starter

▷ Cut and paste your story starter onto the back of your word wall folder for an instant writing idea.

Our Ocean Story Starters

Imagine you turned into an underwater creature. What would you be? Where would you go? What would you wish to learn more about?

Our Ocean Words

folder opens here

Pink Piggy Bank

Our Money Words

Suggested Word List

money
cash
penny
pennies
nickel
dime
quarter
dollar
rich
earn
waste
tax
change
save
spend
credit card
check
buy
allowance
bank
banker
piggy bank

Deposit money words into this little piggy and watch their interest in writing grow and grow!

Cover Decorating Tip

▶ Use a craft knife or sharp scissors to cut the bank's coin slit open. Pleat one or two pieces of paper play money. Slip the money into the slot and glue in place so that some of the money peeks out above the slot. Glue googlie eyes on the pig.

Story Starter

▶ Cut and paste your story starter onto the back of your word wall folder for an instant writing idea.

Our Money Story Starter

Tell about the best ways to save money for something you want. Or, tell about a time you saved money and bought something for yourself or someone else.

fold edge

folder opens here

Our Money Words

Big Red Barn

Our Farm Words

Suggested Word List

chicken

rooster

cow

pig

sheep

goat

horse

duck

dog

cat

feed

milk

ride

hay

grow

harvest

corn

pumpkins

tractor

fields

farmer

scarecrow

Old MacDonald had a farm—and now you have one, too! Use yours to house all the farm words you can raise.

Cover Decorating Tip

▶ Use red and black puff-paints to draw on barn details. In the hayloft, glue on a bit of excelsior to resemble hay.

Story Starters

▶ Cut and paste your story starters onto the back of your word wall folder for instant writing ideas.

Our Farm Story Starters

☼ What's your favorite farm animal? Tell why.

☼ Tell about the chores you'd have to do if you lived on a farm. How do these farm chores compare to the chores you must do now?

Our Farm Words

folder opens here

Cool Car

Pack all your transportation words in this cool car and watch children's writing take off!

Suggested Word List

- car
- truck
- motorcycle
- jeep
- train
- plane
- boat
- taxi
- bike
- bicycle
- bus
- school bus
- helicopter
- travel
- street
- road
- highway
- gas
- airport
- station
- driver
- pilot

Cover Decorating Tip

▶ Cut two circles the same size as the car wheels from file-folder scraps. Use brass fasteners to attach these "turnable tires" to the car shape.

Story Starters

▶ Cut and paste your story starters onto the back of your word wall folder for instant writing ideas.

Our Transportation Story Starters

☼ In your whole life, how many different kinds of vehicles have you ridden in or on?

What vehicle do you especially look forward to trying? Why?

☼ Write about your favorite car trip memory.

fold edge

Our Transportation Words

folder opens here

Birthday Cake

Our Birthday Words

I invite each child to use this tasty word wall to revisit a sweet birthday memory.

Suggested Word List

- party
- invitations
- cake
- icing
- candles
- blow
- hats
- balloons
- napkins
- ice cream
- candy
- treats
- presents
- games
- prizes
- music
- sing
- year
- age
- happy
- clown
- friends

Cover Decorating Tip

▶ Use pink and silver puff-paints to add icing details. Use a sharp knife to trim real birthday candles to fit atop the cake; glue candles in place so that they don't extend too far above the cake shape.

Story Starters

▶ Cut and paste your story starters onto the back of your word wall folder for instant writing ideas.

Our Birthday Story Starters

☀ Write about a favorite birthday memory.

☀ How did the grown-ups in your family celebrate their childhood birthdays?

Our Birthday Words

folder opens here

Terrific Tooth

Our Teeth Words

T ooth tales will abound with the help of this smile-inspired word wall!

Suggested Word List

- tooth
- teeth
- white
- healthy
- wiggle
- jiggle
- loose
- lose
- mouth
- dentist
- toothbrush
- brush
- toothpaste
- floss
- ache
- x-ray
- cavity
- plaque
- check-up
- Tooth Fairy
- pillow
- money

Cover Decorating Tip

▶ Use a waterproof fineline marker to outline cover lettering and Tooth's facial details. Brush entire tooth with a wash of watered-down white glue. While still wet, sprinkle with translucent glitter. Glue on googlie eyes.

Story Starters

▶ Cut and paste your story starters onto the back of your word wall folder for instant writing ideas.

Our Teeth Story Starters

☼ Write about a visit to the dentist.

What does the dentist do first, next, and last?

☼ Make up a story telling about a night in the life of the Tooth Fairy. What does she do with all the baby teeth she collects?

fold edge

folder opens here

Our Teeth Words